The Beatles

The Illustrated Biography

The Beatles

The Illustrated Biography

TIM HILL • ALISON GAUNTLETT • GARETH THOMAS • JANE BENN

Trans
Atlantic
Press

Published by Transatlantic Press
First published in 2008
This edition published in 2009
Reprinted 2011

Transatlantic Press
38 Copthorne Road, Croxley Green, Hertfordshire, WD3 4AQ

© Transatlantic Press
Photographs ©Getty Images

A catalogue record for this book is available from the British Library.
ISBN 978-1-907176-06-7

Printed in China

Contents

Introduction

From the moment John, Paul, George and Ringo began playing together in the summer of 1962, a pop legend was well and truly born. From their Liverpool roots the Beatles crafted their musical talents and took the world of popular music by storm. Driven by the sheer genius of Lennon and McCartney, their compositions caught the imagination of young and old and their sheer presence on stage frequently reduced teenage audiences to tears.

The Beatles were not only talented, they also had the drive and determination to reach their goal. Under the tutelage of manager Brian Epstein the band constantly criss-crossed the country playing a run of 'one-night stands'. Without drawing breath they also squeezed in the growing number of requests for radio and television recordings, not pausing in their touring schedule. Their fame spread rapidly beyond Merseyside and an initial tour of Sweden in 1963 was soon followed by a visit to the States early the following year. America adored the Beatles and after an appearance on *The Ed Sullivan Show* pandemonium followed in their wake.

In June 1964 they embarked on their first major world tour. At every venue a screaming mob of fans desperate to glimpse their idols would be there waiting. Two months later they returned to the States to play in twenty-four cities during a seismic twenty-six day tour. Their albums and singles would automatically shoot to the top of the charts, often breaking sales records before the official release dates. Building on success they branched out into the world of cinema with their first film *A Hard Day's Night,* an instant box office success.

During 1965 the treadmill of playing live and coping with the fans that mobbed them at every venue, the Beatles made a conscious decision to spend more time in the studio and less time on the road. A second world tour took place the following year but on August 29, 1966 at Candlestick Park in San Francisco, they played their last gig. They could now relax a little, build on their business interests and focus on the next album *Sgt. Pepper's Lonely Hearts Club Band.*

However, tensions between the four were beginning to drive the Beatles apart. In the studio they increasingly worked individually rather than collectively and eventually disagreements over music and business interests led each member of the band to actively pursue a solo career. The group parted in 1970 but it was by no means the end of the legend. They were a pop phenomenon that defined the sixties and the Beatles' legacy is still very much alive today.

Part One

Four Lads from Liverpool

John meets Paul

Left: Paul McCartney pictured with his father and his brother, Mike, in 1960. Paul first met John Lennon at the St. Peter's Church fête in Woolton on July 6, 1957. John, then aged sixteen, was already fronting the Quarry Men, who were playing at the fête. Paul, a year younger than John, had gone along to watch. Paul soon impressed John with his guitar skills and was invited to join the group.

Opposite: The following year Paul introduced George Harrison to the band and by February 1958 three out of the final four Beatles (here photographed outside Paul's house) were an established line-up; it was another two years before Ringo Starr joined them. Over the next eighteen months the three found that the path to fame was not straightforward; there were many other performers on the circuit and it was difficult to get gigs. Despite this, the band made its first record by paying 17s 6d to have "That'll Be The Day" cut, with "In Spite Of All The Danger" on the flip-side. This was a McCartney and Harrison song, showing that the boys were writing their own music from the band's earliest days.

Stuart Sutcliffe names The Beatles

The Beatles' first drummer, Pete Best, pictured with the band (opposite: from the left: Pete Best, George Harrison, Paul McCartney, John Lennon). The boys had needed a rhythm section and finally found their drummer just days before they set off for a seven-week stint at the Indra Club in Hamburg, Germany. During a visit to the Casbah Club in West Derby they discovered that the resident band was splitting up and so its drummer, Pete Best, was rapidly auditioned and recruited in time to join them for the Hamburg trip.

At the beginning of 1960 Stuart Sutcliffe, a friend from John's art college, had joined the group to play bass. His musical talent proved to be limited but he fitted the rock 'n' roll image that the band was trying to create. His greatest influence was to suggest that the group change its name. After an initial suggestion of a link to insects, presumably with hopes of mirroring the success of the Crickets, several different names were tried before they finally settled on the Beatles.

Ringo joins the band

Opposite and above: The Beatles performing in one of their first television recordings. In February 1961 the band played the first of nearly three hundred gigs at the Cavern Club in Liverpool and, crucially, in November were seen by record retailer Brian Epstein, who soon became their manager. The following year Epstein approached EMI, where he met producer George Martin. Martin liked what he heard and in June 1962 signed the boys to EMI. George, Paul and John then addressed their concerns about Pete Best's drumming skills and, also unhappy at his refusal to lose his rock 'n' roll quiff, they decided to sack him. Ringo Starr had stood in for Best a few times in Hamburg and the Beatles decided they wanted him as a permanent replacement; so the final line-up was now in place. In September 1962 "Love Me Do"/"PS I Love You" was recorded for release in the UK the following month. The single received some air-play and reached the lower listings in some of the charts, but George Martin felt the band was worth promoting and by the end of 1962 the boys were moving from one level of exposure to another, still playing live at small venues but also receiving opportunities to promote their music through radio and television recordings.

First Silver Record

Above: In April 1963 "Please Please Me" (with "Ask Me Why" on the flip side) earned the Beatles their first silver disk. Released in January 1963, the single quickly reached the top of the UK listings, including those in *Melody Maker* and *New Musical Express*.

Opposite: The group, which was becoming known for its antics, dress up as policemen to avoid fans at the Birmingham Hippodrome. In February 1963 they began their first national tour, booked to support sixteen-year-old Helen Shapiro. Throughout the fourteen performances of the tour, the band worked its way up the bill until it was given the prestigious slot closing the first half of each gig. The boys traveled to the venues by coach with the other supporting acts, and on the journey from Shrewsbury to York John and Paul wrote "From Me To You," which became their next single.

Please Please Me

Above and opposite: The Beatles' popularity and fame increased rapidly, bringing them a cult following as they traveled round the country performing at a different venue almost every night. Media interest also grew and they were regularly asked to pose for official photographs. In March 1963 they began a second British tour supporting the visiting American performers Chris Montez and Tommy Roe.

In the studio in February, during a marathon thirteen-hour session, the Beatles had recorded ten tracks for the forthcoming album *Please Please Me*, keeping up their vocal stamina with throat lozenges and cigarettes. The ten tracks were made up of six cover versions, including "Twist and Shout," and four Lennon and McCartney songs. The fifteen-track album, which included eight of the Beatles' own compositions in all, was released in March 1963 and in May it reached the top of the UK album charts, remaining at No. 1 for an incredible thirty weeks.

Northern Songs

Above: The band appears at the Majestic Ballroom, Birkenhead, for the last time. In February 1963 the boys signed a contract that they were later to regret. Working with publisher Dick James, they agreed to form a company called Northern Songs that would publish all the Lennon and McCartney compositions, with the band owning a fifty percent stake. James owned the other half of the company but was also entitled to a ten percent handling fee. This contract resulted in the loss of millions of pounds in revenue for the Beatles and there was eventually a legal wrangle over the ownership of the company.

Opposite: The four lads mime a drive in a car. They appealed to all generations, largely because of their cheeky but clean-cut image; while teenagers were whipped into a frenzy of hysterical adulation, their parents also enjoyed the band's catchy tunes.

Arrival of the "Fab Four"

Left: The band was now interspersing
concerts with recording session for
the Parlophone label, working with
producer George Martin.

In January 1963 Brian Epstein
had signed a contract with Vee-Jay
Records which allowed the company
to issue Beatles' records in the
United States. "From Me To
You"/"Thank You Girl" was released
Stateside in May 1963 but failed to
make any impression on the *Billboard*
charts.

Opposite: A moment of quiet: during
their British tours screams from the
frenzied audiences often drowned
out the music completely. Regardless
of the order in which acts were billed,
everyone was waiting for the "Fab
Four," as they came to be known.
The Beatles' stamina and
determination was impressive;
staying in cheap accommodation and
spending hours criss-crossing the
country by coach, they kept doggedly
to a punishing schedule in pursuit of
their dream.

Beatlemania at the Palladium

Above and opposite: The *Daily Mirror* coined the phrase "Beatlemania" in a report describing the frenzy that greeted the Beatles when they made a guest appearance on Val Parnell's *Sunday Night at the London Palladium*, playing a four-number set. Watched by a live audience of 2,000, this prestigious TV show also drew weekly television audiences of 15 million. Outside the theater, fans trying to catch a glimpse of their idols brought the West End of London to a standstill, and local police, caught unawares, struggled to control the emotional crowd.

The boys were back on the road for their third tour in May 1963, supporting the American star Roy Orbison and receiving second billing themselves. However, their energy and sheer magnetism left no-one in any doubt about who was the greater draw. "From Me To You" shot to the top of the UK charts on its release in April, the first of eleven singles to go straight to No. 1. "She Loves You"/"I'll Get You," recorded at Abbey Road in July 1963, was released in August and became the band's first million-selling single, reaching the top of the charts on two separate occasions.

Ready, Steady, Go!

Above: The group managed to find time for a brief, one-week rest at the end of September 1963 and early in October they met up again at the Star Steak House in Shaftesbury Avenue, London. That evening they made their debut on the television pop show *Ready, Steady, Go!*, broadcast live from Television House. After miming to three songs they were interviewed by host Keith Fordyce and singer Dusty Springfield.

Opposite: Time for more official photo calls. In September 1963 the Beatles were presented with the Top Vocal Group of the Year award at the Variety Club Awards lunch held at the Savoy Hotel, London. They spent the rest of the afternoon watching the Rolling Stones; an article in that day's *Daily Mirror* described the group as "Four frenzied Little Lord Fauntleroys who are making £50,000 every week." Meanwhile, in the United States "She Loves You"/"I'll Get You" was released on Swan 4152 but again failed to make the *Billboard* listings. The US market was to remain unconquered for a while.

Yeah, yeah, yeah, yeah

Opposite: A rare, peaceful moment for Paul McCartney at Stockholm airport. The band began recording its next album, *With The Beatles*, during the summer of 1963 and at the end of the final day of recording in October, the boys flew to Sweden to begin their first foreign tour. Back in Britain "She Loves You" had already sold half a million copies, making it the bestselling UK single ever, a record it held for fourteen years. The characteristic opening drum roll and the falsetto "oooos" and "yeah, yeah, yeahs" came to symbolize that summer.

Above: A chance to read fan mail in their Swedish dressing room. During the eight-day tour the band continued its usual rigorous schedule, playing nine houses at six different venues. While the boys were away, George Martin finished the final mix of the new album *With The Beatles*.

Beatles abroad

Opposite: A chance for a bemused Swedish boy to meet the band. On their first day in the country the Beatles took part in a radio interview at a studio in Stockholm and also made a recording for the Swedish television show *Drop In*. This was followed by an appearance at a record shop in Boras, signing records for delighted fans. Flying back into London airport, they were greeted by thousands of fans.

Final Cavern appearance

Above: Even in their hotel suite in Sweden the boys continued to work, experimenting with new lyrics and harmonies. That summer the Beatles were also given the chance to extend their radio appearances with their own show, *Pop Go The Beatles*, which ran for thirteen weeks. On August 3, they played their final set at the Cavern Club; their final fee was £300, a marked increase on the sum of £5 for their first appearance!

Opposite: As part of a six-week British tour, the group made their only appearances in Ireland in November 1963, playing two nights in Dublin and Belfast. Brian Epstein had just agreed a deal with United Artists to make a movie about the group and so during the tour the Beatles were shadowed by screenwriter Alun Owen. The movie was released the following year as *A Hard Day's Night*.

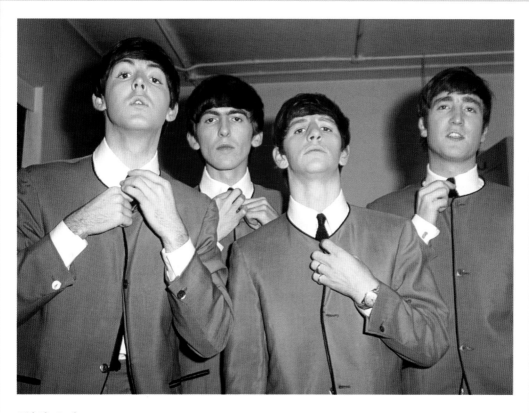

With The Beatles

Opposite: George Harrison, on the other side of the camera for a change. The band's new album, *With The Beatles*, was released at the end of November 1963. The Beatles, dedicated to producing quality work, insisted that the album contain new work and were insistent on their choice of album cover, despite criticism from Brian Epstein and EMI. The iconic cover shot of the four was captured in subdued lighting in a Bournemouth hotel corridor by Robert Freeman.

Above: A quick adjustment to their new suits. In December 1963 a new single, "I Want To Hold Your Hand"/"This Boy," was released; it was the first of their singles to receive over a million advance orders. A year later it became their first No. 1 hit in the United States, reaching the top slot in the *Billboard* chart. The British tour, which had seen the boys play at different venues virtually every night, ended in mid-December 1963, but they immediately began work on their Christmas show, which opened at the Astoria Cinema, Finsbury Park, London, on Christmas Eve and ran until January 11, 1964.

Making plans for America

Above and opposite: The band was now attracting great media attention; on November 3 they appeared on the *Ken Dodd Show*, which was broadcast live in the afternoon, and they went on immediately to make their first appearance on the radio program *The Public Ear*. Meanwhile, Brian Epstein was in the States, meeting Ed Sullivan to arrange an appearance by the Beatles on his TV show. Back in England the album *With The Beatles* had received advance orders of 300,000 but after its release soon passed the half million mark and had sold over one million copies by 1965.

A Royal performance

Opposite and above: In November 1963 the band achieved another first, with an invitation to perform at the *Royal Variety Show*. Billed seventh out of nineteen acts, they spent the previous day in rehearsals before performing in front of the Queen Mother, Princess Margaret, and Lord Snowdon. It was during their set that John, ever the comedian, asked the audience to clap or, if they were in the expensive seats, to "rattle their jewelry."

Composers of the year

Above: The Beatles ended 1963 in a whirl of activity. In the middle of the eleven-day run of their Christmas show, the band recorded an appearance on the music panel show *Juke Box Jury*. By now the album *With The Beatles* was at the top of the UK charts, where it remained for twenty-one weeks, and Lennon and McCartney were named the best composers of the year by the critic of the London *Times*.

Opposite: The Beatles dressed in boaters and stripy blazers for their appearance on the Christmas edition of the *Morecambe and Wise Show*. After performing in several sketches and singing three numbers, the boys donned these outfits to sing "Moonlight Bay."

US single release

Opposite and above: The band making its second appearance on *Val Parnell's Sunday Night at the London Palladium* on January 12, 1964, in a line-up including compere Bruce Forsyth, singer Alma Cogan and comedian Dave Allen. The fee for this appearance on the show reflected the change in their status since their first appearance three months earlier; then they were paid £250, but this time they received £1,000.

The band was also now poised for recognition in the United States, where they were still largely unknown. EMI had pressed its subsidiary Capitol to release "I Want To Hold Your Hand," and the company's executives, mostly unaware of this new group, planned to release the single in the new year. However, management moves to raise the Beatles' US profile were overtaken by events; whenWWDC, a Washington radio station, played an imported copy of the single the feedback prompted the company to rush out the single on Boxing Day. Almost overnight, it seemed, the Beatles' ambition of conquering the international market—including the biggest prize of all, the USA—was within their grasp.

Top of the Pops

Above: The very first episode of the TV program *Top of the Pops*, presented by DJ Jimmy Savile, was broadcast on January 1, 1964. The Beatles joined the Rolling Stones, Dusty Springfield, and the Dave Clark Five on the show, which ended with a performance of their No. 1 hit "I Want To Hold Your Hand."

Opposite: The band sign autographs in Paris after flying into Le Bouget airport on January 14, 1964. They began their visit with a performance at the Cinema Cyrano in Versailles. Toward the end of their stay at the George V Hotel in Paris, they were given a huge boost by the news that "I Want to Hold Your Hand"/"I Saw Her Standing There" had reached the top of the American Cash Box chart – less than three weeks after its release in the United States.

Le Beatles

Opposite: Paul McCartney waves from a taxi on the Champs Elysees as the band prepares to begin a three-week run at the Olympia Theatre, Paris, France's top music venue. The Beatles experienced a unexpected return of freedom in Paris as "Beatlemania" had not yet gripped the French, so security was less of a problem than in the UK. France, a completely different market from Britain as far as musical tastes were concerned, was notoriously difficult to conquer.

Right: The band continue to enjoy their new-found liberty as they pose between two statues in Paris. Only a few fans asked for their autographs, and the novelty of sightseeing without being pursued was a welcome relief. As ever, the band was committed to a daunting schedule, performing two or three times a day and only taking two rest days. Part of one performance, which included five Beatles' songs as well as material from other artists, was broadcast live on the French radio station Europe.

"Sie Liebt Dich"

Opposite and above: The band, with its manager Brian Epstein, enjoy the luxury of their suite at the George V Hotel in Paris. John and Paul were under pressure to compose songs for their new album as well as the forthcoming movie *A Hard Day's Night* while on the French tour. Although the two had always been accomplished at writing songs between concerts whatever their surroundings, the plush Paris hotel suite was a marked improvement on the back of a bus, where they had penned some of their original work.

While in France the band recorded "I Want To Hold Your Hand" and "She Loves You" in German to appeal to the German market. Although neither George Martin nor the four boys believed that translation was necessary, they agreed to the request and on January 29 "Komm, Gib Mir Deine Hand" and "Sie Liebt Dich" were recorded at the EMI Pathé Marconi Studios, together with "Can't Buy Me Love" in English. These were the only two foreign-language recordings ever made by the Beatles.

World-wide attention

Opposite: The band played to packed houses at the Olympia Theatre but the reviews in the French press were mixed. Comments ranged from remarks about their unusual style of dress and the strange way they held their guitars, to more positive responses about their excellent sense of rhythm. The Beatles remained philosophical about the disparate opinions, concentrating on writing material for their new album. The ambience of the George V Hotel, complete with a piano installed for their stay, was conducive to composition and they produced a greater number of songs than expected. This affected plans for their third album; instead of including

seven new numbers and some old compositions, an LP with thirteen new songs was now envisaged.

Above: The French singer Sylvie Vartan was one of their co-stars at the Olympia Theater. Following the completion of the tour the Beatles returned to England on February 5, unperturbed by the mixed reviews from the French press. However, they were surprised to learn that unflattering comments had appeared in the newspapers in Moscow—not only the first references to the group in the Soviet press, but also the first-ever coverage of a British pop group!

"England's phenomenal pop combo"

Above: Paul signs an autograph for a member of staff at London airport as the band prepares to fly to the United States on February 7, 1964 to make its American debut. Any doubts the Beatles might have had about succeeding in the United States must have been laid to rest by their reception at John F. Kennedy airport, which was as frenzied and chaotic as any in Britain.

Opposite: John's wife, Cynthia, accompanied him on the flight to America. As the success of the group continued, she was envied by women all over the world. So sudden was the popularity of the Beatles in the States that Capitol had hastily to contract out the record pressing of "I Want To Hold Your Hand" to RCA and Columbia to meet demand. The album *Meet the Beatles!*, released Stateside in January 1964, was subtitled "The first album by England's phenomenal pop combo."

New York, New York

Above: The "Fab Four" landing at John F. Kennedy airport, where they were showered with jelly beans and candy kisses. By the time they reached New York, "Beatlemania" was in full swing as the local radio stations went to town reporting on the band's arrival. The airport was filled with thousands of screaming fans, all desperate to see the group, and fans lined the entire route into New York. The boys needed a police escort to the Plaza Hotel, where they stayed during their visit.

Opposite: The boys enjoying a few quiet moments away from their fans. The police smuggled them out of their hotel for a visit to New York's Central Park, where they rode in a horse-drawn carriage. All other attempts at sightseeing ended in chaos. The extent to which the city entered into the spirit of their visit was exemplified by the New York Radio Station, which played only Beatles' records, interspersed with facts and news items about the group. One such bulletin reported George's problem with a sore throat, which forced him to miss most of a rehearsal for a television show.

Live on Ed Sullivan

Above: The Beatles first appeared live on American TV on the *Ed Sullivan Show* on February 9 in front of a studio audience of 728 people. Sullivan had negotiated a very competitive deal, securing two live appearances and one recorded set for $10,000. This was well below the going rate but Brian Epstein had shrewdly perceived that the exposure the band would receive was worth the low fee.

Opposite: A reported 50,000 people applied for tickets for the show – more than for any of Elvis' three appearances in 1958. Over 70 million TV viewers watched as the band opened the show with "All My Loving." The boys played a total of five songs on this first appearance, including "Till There Was You" and "She Loves You" and both sides of their US No. 1 single, "I Want To Hold Your Hand" and "I Saw Her Standing There."

First US concert

Opposite and above: Following their appearance on the *Ed Sullivan Show* the band traveled to Washington DC. They had to take a train as their flight was canceled because of bad weather, but their arrival in this city was a much calmer affair than it had been in New York. A few thousand fans turned up at the station to greet them but there was no repeat of the scenes at John F. Kennedy airport; they were even able to see the sights of the city in relative peace.

On February 11, the Beatles played their first live US concert at the Washington Coliseum for 8,000 fans – the biggest show they had ever performed. The Coliseum was an unusual venue for a concert but the theater was chosen because of its huge revolving stage. This was rotated to give the entire audience a good view of the band as they played, though it meant that the group had to reposition themselves at regular intervals.

Capital success

Left: George passes the time reading a paper on the train ride to Washington DC. An uncomfortable problem arose at the Washington concert, where a shower of jelly beans rained down on the band. The American press had reported that George particularly enjoyed eating jelly babies, a popular confection in Britain but unknown in the States. The fans took this to mean the much harder jelly bean! But being pelted with jelly beans did not detract from the Beatles' performance, regarded by many as the high point of their touring career.

Opposite: A make-up artist works on George as the group prepares to rehearse for their second appearance on the *Ed Sullivan Show* in Miami. Their first appearance on the TV show was believed to be responsible for the huge interest in the subsequent live concerts at Carnegie Hall in New York.

Carnegie Hall

Above: The Beatles returned from their successful performance in Washington to give two live performances at Carnegie Hall, New York. Impresario Sid Bernstein had taken a risk and booked the band to play the venue before he had even heard their music, borrowing money in order to put down a deposit. The demand for tickets was so great that many seats were added to the stage, while thousands of disappointed fans gathered outside. Mrs Nelson Rockefeller, wife of the New York State Governor, was one of a minority of adults in the audience and was allocated a seat in a prized position next to the band.

Opposite: Such was the success of the shows that Sid Bernstein tried unsuccessfully to persuade Brian Epstein to add a last-minute concert at Madison Square Garden. A US tour was already planned for later in the summer, but, to the frustration of American fans, the Beatles only played three concerts on this first trip.

Enjoying the Florida sunshine

Opposite and above: The "Fab Four" taking a well-earned rest in the Florida sunshine, enjoying the sun, sea, and sand at Miami beach after the cold and snow of New York. When they flew in, several thousand dollars worth of damage was done to windows and doors of the airport by the thousands of fans clamoring for a glimpse of the foursome. The Beatles' only formal commitment during their Miami break was their second live appearance on the *Ed Sullivan Show*. Apart from this engagement and their usual round of media interviews, the band was free to enjoy the warm Florida weather. The four were tempted into the sea on many occasions – usually followed by the press and their adoring fans.

Knockout US record sales

Opposite: As the Beatles continued to relax, their album *Meet The Beatles!* was in huge demand in the United States, selling as quickly as their No. 1 single "I Want To Hold Your Hand"; the single's eventual total sales were over five million copies at a time when records rarely sold even one million. The LP had reached the No. 1 spot in the US album charts two days earlier, a position it held for eleven weeks.

Right: Cassius Clay pretends to knock out all four Beatles. During their time in Florida, the Beatles visited contender Cassius Clay at the Fifth Street Gym, Miami, where he was training for his eagerly awaited heavyweight title fight with champion Sonny Liston.

Reaching 70 million across America

Opposite: The Beatles' second appearance on the *Ed Sullivan Show* was broadcast from the Deauville Hotel before an audience of 3,500. Mitzi Gaynor nominally topped the bill, and the television viewing figures again reached 70 million as an estimated 22,445,000 homes tuned in throughout America.

Above: The Beatles performed six songs: "She Loves You," "This Boy," "All My Loving," "I Saw Her Standing There," "From Me To You," and "I Want To Hold Your Hand." This set was almost identical to the songs they had played on their first appearance, apart from the substitution of "This Boy" for "Till There Was You" and the addition of "From Me To You." The show was broadcast again four days later.

Relaxing in Miami

Opposite and above: As the band relaxed by the pool in their Miami hotel, discussions were taking place about which song to release next. Capitol was keen to distribute the Beatles' version of "Roll Over Beethoven" as a follow-up to "I Want To Hold Your Hand," while George Martin favored "Can't Buy Me Love." The record producer won the day and "Can't Buy Me Love" was the next single released by Capitol, quickly becoming the Beatles' second No. 1 single in the United States, a position it held for 13 consecutive weeks. Even before the "Fab Four" left Florida, Brian Epstein was being bombarded with lucrative offers for the band's return. As well as the many offers, he had already received $253,000 in royalties from Capitol for just one month's record sales. However, there were pressing engagements in the UK and it was six months before the Beatles returned to America.

End of the first US tour

Opposite and above: A last swim for Paul before leaving Miami. The Beatles left Florida on February 21 and made a brief stop in New York before flying back to Britain. They spent just over two weeks in the United States but in that short time they had taken the country by storm. Three concerts and two live appearances on the *Ed Sullivan Show* had completely changed American perceptions of the band.

Big Night Out back in the UK

Above and opposite: The group records *Big Night Out* with comedians Mike and Bernie Winters at the ABC Television studios in Teddington. Their flight back from the United States had landed at 8.10 a.m. the previous day at London airport, where the BBC was waiting to film their arrival; their interview with BBC sports presenter David Coleman was considered of such significance that it was shown in the middle of that afternoon's edition of the sports program *Grandstand*. The BBC was only one of several media organizations to film their arrival, and Pathé News later produced a special report called *Beatles Welcome Home*, with reporter Bob Danvers-Walker narrating the day's events in footage destined for cinemas throughout the country. Brian Matthews, presenter of the BBC radio program *Saturday Club*, also held a brief telephone interview with the boys which was broadcast in that morning's edition.

In His Own Write

Above and opposite: Shots taken during the filming of the Beatles' movie *A Hard Day's Night*. On March 2, 1964, after hastily obtaining Equity cards that morning, the four band members gathered at Paddington railway station to begin filming. Using a screenplay written by Alun Owen, the movie was a frenetic tale of forty-eight hours in the life of the band, although without the drinking, smoking and bad language that was part of their daily lives. The shoot lasted eight weeks but the movie's title was not settled until filming was nearing completion. The title came from a classic Ringo one-liner, coined on a day of filming that began at 6 a.m. and continued well into the night. John used the phrase in his book *In His Own Write*, published while the movie was being filmed, but credited Ringo as the source.

George meets Pattie

Opposite: Actress Anna Quayle peeping over John's shoulder. Although it was agreed that the movie would not include any love interest, George was instantly attracted to model Pattie Boyd, who was playing one of the schoolgirls on the train.

Above: Pattie Boyd attends to George's locks while other co-stars from the movie look after John, Paul, and Ringo. When George plucked up the courage to ask Pattie for a date, she refused as she was already in a relationship. But he persisted and she ended her existing relationship to begin dating George. They attempted to keep the relationship a secret, but the media found them out during a vacation in Ireland with John and Cynthia. On one occasion Pattie and Cynthia, dressed as maids, were sneaked out of a hotel in laundry baskets.

Showbusiness personalities of the year

Above: The politician Harold Wilson presenting the Beatles with the Royal Variety Club Award for Showbusiness Personalities of 1963 at the Dorchester Hotel, London. Wilson, whose constituency was near Liverpool, was keen to be pictured with the band, seeing them as a great vote-catcher who would enhance his public image. Taking every photo opportunity, Wilson posed with the band and responded well to their banter. Later that year he won the general election, becoming prime minister for six years, and during his time in

office he recommended the boys for the honors they received from the Queen (the MBE—Member of the Order of the British Empire) and he was also mentioned, along with his successor Edward Heath, in their single "Taxman."

Opposite: The band traveled north of the border in late April 1964, to play in Glasgow and Edinburgh. A photo call with the boys playing the drums and bagpipes gave them the ideal opportunity to promote their visit.

Fourteen releases in the US charts

Opposite: Their next single, "Can't Buy Me Love"/"You Can't Do That," was released in March 1964 in Britain and the United States, where two million copies were sold within the first week. On April 4 the single reached No. 1 in America, putting the Beatles in possession of the first five places in the Hot 100 chart, a record that has still not been broken; the next four places were occupied by "Twist and Shout," "She Loves You," "I Want To Hold Your Hand," and "Please Please Me", and there were seven other releases further down the listings. A week later, two more singles joined the charts, giving the band fourteen releases in the US charts. Some of these tracks were not released as singles in Britain as the band felt that they were more suitable material for an album.

Above: As filming of *A Hard Day's Night* finished at the end of April, the band went straight into rehearsals for *Around The Beatles*, a television special. Their set included their recent single "Can't Buy Me Love" and several earlier hits before the boys embarked on drama. Dressed in Elizabethan costumes they took part in a skit based on Shakespeare's *A Midsummer Night's Dream*, with Paul taking the role of Pyramus, John playing Thisbe, George as Moonshine, and Ringo as the Lion.

Around the Beatles

Above: Paul meets his waxwork model at Madame Tussaud's in Baker Street, London, in April 1964. Models of all four Beatles went on display that summer and proved a real asset to the museum as fans poured in to see them. Three years later the mannequins were used on the *Sgt. Pepper's Lonely Hearts Club Band* album cover, dressed in military style.

Opposite: The band surrounded by adoring fans during rehearsals for *Around The Beatles*.

Bestselling author

Opposite: John was a guest of honor at the Foyles Literary Lunch at the Dorchester Hotel in April 1964, where he was seated next to composer and lyricist Lionel Bart. John was described as "an inveterate scribbler with a passion for word play, quirky turns of phrase, nonsense verse and anarchic humor." His first book, *In His Own Write*, published in March, was adored by both readers and critics, selling out immediately.

Right: John had left the set of *A Hard Day's Night* to attend the lunch and in his absence director Richard Lester finished filming the scene that accompanied "Can't Buy Me Love," the reason why only three Beatles appear in this section of the movie.

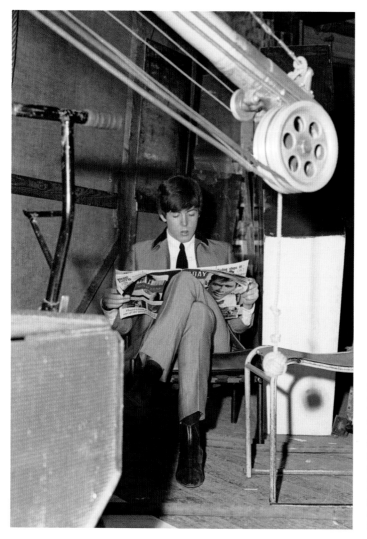

Filming A Hard Day's Night

Left: Paul taking the opportunity to read a magazine backstage at the Scala Theatre, London. The interior scenes for *A Hard Day's Night* were filmed there, with some exterior scenes shot around the theater in Charlotte Mews and Tottenham Street.

Opposite: The band preparing for another television recording. On April 4 "Can't Buy Me Love"/"You Can't Do That" also reached the top of the UK charts, matching the single's success in the States, and remained there for three weeks.

The Fab Four take a break

Opposite: The boys pictured during the filming of *A Hard Day's Night*. In May they were finally able to take a much-needed vacation, though it was not a lengthy one as they began their first world tour in June. Needing a break from the relentless pressures of their fame and the media, John and Cynthia with George and Pattie Boyd traveled to Honolulu, while Paul and girlfriend Jane Asher, and Ringo and his girlfriend Maureen Cox, opted for a stay in the Virgin Islands. Code names were adopted in an effort to maintain secrecy about their whereabouts and ensure some privacy.

Above: Paul celebrating his 22nd birthday at a party in Sydney, Australia. In April the boys had broken another US record when *The Beatles' Second Album* replaced *Meet The Beatles!* at the top of the US charts, the first time a No. 1 album had been supplanted by another from the same artist. Many of the tracks from *The Beatles' Second Album* had been released in Britain on the *With The Beatles* album the previous year.

Beatles down under

Opposite: The band gives Ringo Starr the bumps on his 24th birthday in July. In June 1964 they embarked on a month-long world tour, spending most of the time in Australia and New Zealand. They were the first major artists to visit Australia and the reception in Sydney dwarfed the scenes in America. Ringo Starr had been hospitalized with severe tonsilitis and pharyngitis before the band left, so it was session drummer Jimmy Nicol who emerged from the plane when they arrived in Australia. Over a quarter of a million fans lined the streets in Adelaide in the hope of glimpsing their idols.

Above: The reunited "Fab Four" at London airport after their triumphant return from Australia. Ringo Starr had joined the tour at Melbourne, only two days later than planned. He had left England without the necessary papers but Australian officials waived this formality, another indication of the band's stature by this time. An over-helpful policeman had tried to escort Ringo into his hotel on his shoulders, a plan that failed when he was dropped into the hands of the ecstatic waiting fans.

Twenty-five-day tour of America

Opposite: Black ties for the band and Brian Epstein as they attend the world premiere of *A Hard Day's Night* at the London Pavilion on July 6. Four days later the album accompanying the movie was released in the UK, along with the single "A Hard Day's Night"/"Things We Said Today." That day the band flew to Liverpool for the movie's northern premiere. Fans poured onto the streets to welcome the local heroes as they drove through the city to the Town Hall for a civic reception. These scenes were repeated in the evening, when the movie premiered at the Odeon Cinema, Liverpool; the press were out in force and footage was distributed worldwide.

Above: Cigarettes for Paul and Ringo during a press conference held after their arrival in the United States. In August the boys left Britain for a 25-day tour of America. There was little need for publicity; concert tickets sold out immediately on release, and fans turned out in force wherever they went, regardless of the time of day—in San Francisco a crowd of 9,000 awaited them. The crowds were so huge that eventually the boys were forced to travel straight from the plane to the concert venues for their own safety and that of the public.

US tour kicks off

Above and Opposite: The Beatles at the Convention Center, Las Vegas. The band's American tour kicked off at Cow Palace in San Francisco and included the Righteous Brothers as one of the support acts. After performing to an audience of 17,000 the boys left immediately for the airport, landing at Las Vegas in the early hours of the following morning. Two houses were played at the Convention Center before they traveled to Seattle for the next day's shows.

Police were needed to protect the band from their hysterical fans in Las Vegas. During the tour there were several occasions when the fans' behavior was potentially dangerous. In Cleveland a crash barrier broke and the police had to stop the show, ordering the Beatles off the stage until order was restored and the authorities were confident that the concert could continue safely.

Breaking show-business records

Above: John struggles to hear a question at a US press conference. The band had intended to stay at the Plaza Hotel for their New York show but the hotel refused to accommodate them, having learnt by now what a security headache this would present. Instead the Beatles stayed at the Delmonico, where Ed Sullivan lived. While there they received a visit from Bob Dylan, who would have a significant influence on their lyrics in the future, telling the band to "Listen to the words, man." During their time in the United States the Beatles clocked up 15,000 miles, broke several show-business records and earned in excess of £1 million.

Opposite: A rare moment of relaxation as the boys fish from their room at the Edgewater Inn in Seattle before playing at the Coliseum later that evening. The tour closed in New York on August 20 with a charity performance in aid of the United Cerebral Palsy of New York City and Retarded Infant Services.

Family Man

Left: A quiet family moment for John, his wife Cynthia and their son Julian, born in April 1963. They had just bought Kenwood House in Surrey for £20,000 and subsequently spent £40,000 on renovations. It was a lonely existence for Cynthia and Julian as John was away so much; only nineteen days after their return from the United States the band set off on another tour of Britain.

Opposite: This British tour saw the Beatles' return to playing at provincial cinemas for much smaller returns. It was a marked contrast to the mammoth venues of the summer's US tour, but Brian Epstein and the band were determined to honor previous bookings. The tour began on October 9 in Bradford and, in a frenetic race around the country, the band played a total of fifty-four houses in twenty-seven days. The tour ended with a concert at the Colston Hall, Bristol, on November 10. Although rest days were scheduled these tended to be spent at the Abbey Road studio, completing the recordings of their forthcoming single and album.

Touring the UK

Above: Three members of the band admire the "I love George" cushion sent by a devoted fan. The November 1964 general election occurred during the band's British tour and the boys were playing at Stockton-on-Tees on polling day. Afterwards they admitted that they had made no attempt to register for a postal vote and so had not voted. Paul was quoted as saying, "We don't care a lot about politics," with John adding "We have been away from Liverpool so long we've forgotten which constituency we are in. It's a load of rubbish anyway."

Opposite: John fooling around in his garden in Surrey during a photo shoot, his hat adorned with dead fern fronds. In October the band had a much-needed respite from touring and took advantage of it to record seven songs, including "I Feel Fine" and six tracks for their new album.

First million-copy LP

Above: The boys hold a press conference at the Odeon Cinema in Leeds. During the tour the press began to suggest that the band's popularity was waning, claiming that there were empty seats at an early concert in Bradford. These suggestions were contradicted by the success of the Beatles' next single, "I Feel Fine," and the album *Beatles for Sale*; each received over half a million advance orders, achieving Silver records three weeks and four weeks, respectively, before their release dates. Meanwhile, *With The Beatles*, the album released November 1963, became the first British LP to sell a million copies by 1965.

Opposite: The band pictured in their dressing room preparing for that evening's show at the De Monfort Hall in Leicester. In November the Decca A&R man Dick Rowe countered the media's murmurs about the band, denying that the Beatles' popularity was falling and pointing out that their music was moving towards quieter, more melodic harmonies.

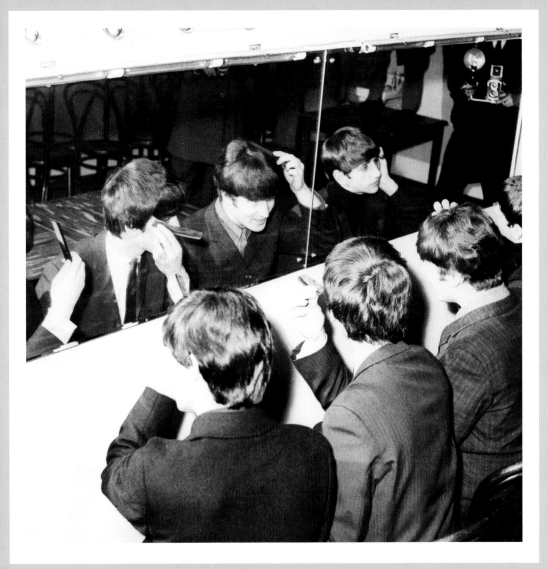

Back to Liverpool

Above: A card game in the dressing room prior to a concert. The band's performances on this tour included one at the Empire Theatre, Liverpool, their first performance there for nearly a year.

Opposite: During the tour it was announced that the Beatles had won five Ivor Novello Awards, including one for Most Outstanding Contribution to Music. In early November two EPs, *Extracts From The Album A Hard Day's Night*, were released in Britain.

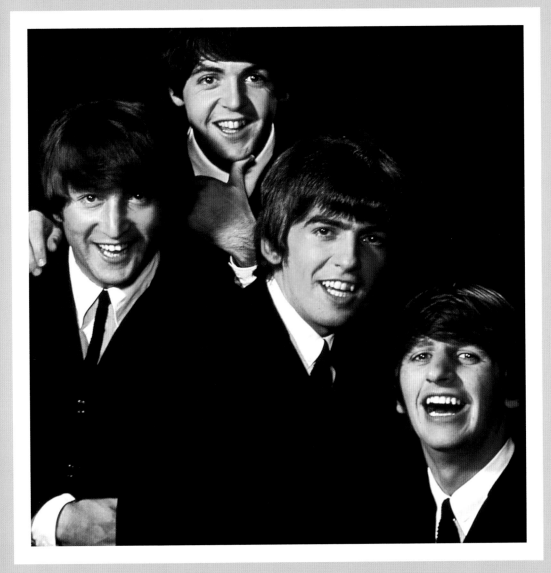

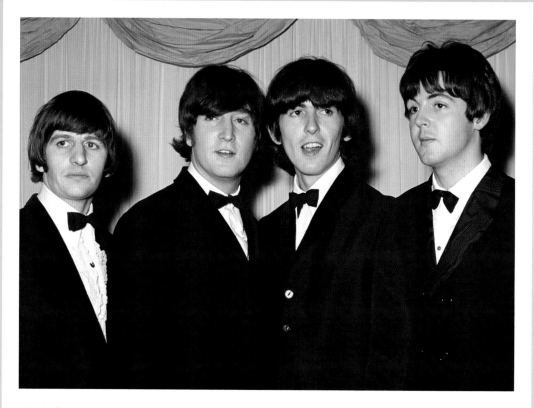

Touring becomes "a drag"

Above: Black ties for the band. During the final stages of UK the tour the magazine *Newsweek* aired rumors that the Beatles were fed up with touring and also with each other, and speculated that they might follow Elvis Presley's example and focus on television and movies. The *Daily Mirror* took up the story, agreeing that the boys were tired of touring and that "Beatlemania" was coming to an end.

Opposite: Despite the pressure from the media and their grueling schedules, the boys' humor and sense of the

ridiculous was ever present. Brian Epstein had immediately countered the media reports, saying, "Nonsense, nonsense, nonsense." He agreed that the band might play fewer concerts in the future but said they had no intention of giving up live performing. He stated that the group was still very popular and that the boys felt a strong sense of duty toward their fans. George agreed, and was quoted as saying, "We love the fans, but tours like this are a drag."

Ringo goes to hospital

Opposite: George pulls on Ringo's arm to stop him escaping as the band continue to lark around. On December 2, as a consequence of his illness earlier in the year, Ringo was admitted to University College Hospital, London, to have his tonsils removed. Rehearsals had already begun for the forthcoming *Another Beatles Christmas Show* but fortunately the performances were not due to start until Christmas Eve, by which time he had recovered.

Above: The band on stage once again. The venue for *Another Beatles Christmas Show*, which combined interviews, songs, and comedy, was the Odeon Cinema in Hammersmith, West London. The band played thirty-eight houses between December 24 and January 16, giving a special performance on December 29, the proceeds from which were donated to charity. The Yardbirds were included on the bill, giving the band the opportunity to meet Eric Clapton for the first time, and the year closed with the boys appearing on *Top of the Pops '64*.

Drive my car

Above: 1965 began well, with the Beatles topping the charts on both sides of the Atlantic with their latest single, "I Feel Fine," and with their second run of Christmas variety shows over by mid-January, there was then time for a well-earned break. John and Cynthia decided to head to St. Moritz, Switzerland, to ski with George Martin and his wife, while Paul opted for the much warmer climes of Tunisia. George meanwhile, returned to Liverpool to attend his brother's wedding, and just days later, on February 11, Ringo married his long-term girlfriend Maureen Cox in London. John, George, and Brian Epstein were in attendance, but Paul was unable to make it back for the seemingly impromptu affair.

Opposite: Shortly afterwards, the Beatles returned to the studio to begin work on their next album, with John somehow managing to find time to pass his driving test between sessions.

Help!

Opposite and above: Just a week after beginning work on their new album, the boys were waved off by crowds of well-wishers at London Airport, as they headed for New Providence in the Bahamas to begin shooting their second feature film. The movie was given the working title *Beatles 2*, although it would be re-titled *Help!* by the time of its release. As with *A Hard Day's Night*, *Help!* was directed by Richard Lester, but as the choice of location revealed, the budget for this film was considerably larger, which also allowed for the picture to be shot in color. Significantly, *Help!* would also differ in terms of style, for whilst *A Hard Day's Night* had taken the Beatles' own experiences as a springboard for the plot, *Help!* had originally been scripted as a madcap caper intended for Peter Sellers, and as a result, the boys would be almost entirely immersed in a fantasy world from start to finish.

Filming in the in the Bahamas

Opposite: As filming on *Help!* commenced in the Bahamas, the Beatles were undoubtedly pleased to be swapping a cold British winter for tropical warmth and sunshine. However, they would be forced to spend much of their time in the shade to avoid sunburn, or even a tan, which might play havoc with continuity, as many of the film's earlier scenes would be shot in Britain in the weeks to come.

Above: The Bahamas shoot commenced on February 23 with the boys emerging fully-clothed from the swimming pool at the Nassau Beach Hotel, and would end around two weeks later, during which time the Beatles were expected to be filming from 8.30 am in the morning until 5.30 pm in the evening each day. In practice however, most of the action had to be captured in the morning, as the boys had begun to indulge their appetite for marijuana at this time, which often rendered them less than focused by the afternoon.

Ticket To Ride

Opposite and right: Back in Britain, filming would continue in Twickenham in March, with a number of sequences being shot at the famed and familiar Twickenham Film Studios, although the film's opening scenes, which showed the Fab Four arriving home to their adjacent suburban properties, were shot on location in nearby Ailsa Avenue in early April.

Around this time, the Beatles released their next single, "Ticket To Ride," which they had actually recorded two months earlier, even before filming began, but which was always intended for the *Help!* soundtrack album. The song represented a major departure from the straightforward, feel-good pop of their earlier singles, with its darker, more brooding lyrics and more complex, irregular sound, but nevertheless, it would provide the boys with a sixth consecutive transatlantic No 1. On April 10, they recorded a mimed performance of "Ticket To Ride," to be aired on *Top of the Pops*.

All-Star Concert

Opposite and above: Wearing the same fawn-colored jackets that they had donned the previous day for the *Top Of The Pops* recording, and in which they would famously later appear at Shea Stadium, New York, the Beatles attended the *New Musical Express* 1964-65 Annual Poll-Winners' All-Star Concert at the Empire Pool Wembley on April 11, where they would be presented with their awards by American crooner Tony Bennett. They also performed five songs for the 10,000-strong audience, including their most recent chart-toppers,

"I Feel Fine" and "Ticket To Ride."Later that evening, The Beatles appeared live on ABC Television's *The Eamonn Andrews Show*, where they discussed the making of their current movie, before miming to "Ticket To Ride" and the B-side, "Yes It Is." Two days later, more awards were headed the Beatles' way, with the announcement that they had won Grammy Awards for Best New Artist and Best Performance by a Vocal Group.

Austrian Alps

Left and opposite: In addition to filming in the sunny Bahamas and suburban London, the Beatles also spent a week shooting on the snowy slopes near Obertauern, in the Austrian Alps, where they and their doubles were to film sleigh-ride, ski-lift, and curling sequences, amongst others. It was at this time that *Eight Arms to Hold You* was announced as the new provisional title for the Beatles' second movie, although this would soon come to be regarded as too unwieldy, and replaced with the short, succinct, *Help!*. This not only seemed to fit the plot of the film, with the boys attempting to prevent Ringo's capture by an Eastern cult, but provided the Beatles, and John in particular, with the opportunity to articulate just how beleaguered they had become in real life. "Help!" John's heartfelt, pleading title track, would be released as the next single in July, accompanying the opening of the film.

Dylan's influence

Above and opposite: As May began, the Beatles found themselves filming for a few days on Salisbury Plain, Wiltshire, before relocating to the more hospitable surroundings of Cliveden House in Buckinghamshire on May 10. Most of the filming took place inside, with Cliveden's sumptuous interior being used to represent that of Buckingham Palace in the movie, although some scenes were shot outside on the terrace, where the boys were also able to relax during breaks between scenes.

The previous evening, the Beatles had attended the Royal Albert Hall in London to watch a performance by Bob Dylan, whose song-writing was proving to be a major influence on John Lennon at this time. However, returning to London for a session on the evening of the 10th, the boys opted to record two of John's favorite up-tempo rock-and-roll tracks by American artist Larry Williams, including "Dizzy Miss Lizzy," which would feature on the forthcoming *Help!* LP.

Completing Help!

Left and opposite: When the Beatles finished filming at Cliveden House on May 11, they had in fact completed shooting *Help!*, although the crew would spend a further day filming on location in London, and the boys would be required to return to Twickenham Film Studios to complete numerous overdubs during the post-production stages.

Toward the end of the month, just after the Grammy Awards ceremony was broadcast in the US, "Ticket To Ride" topped the *Billboard* chart, and on May 26, the Beatles recorded a special two-hour feature for BBC radio's Light Programme, entitled *The Beatles (Invite You To Take A Ticket To Ride)*. The show was broadcast on Bank Holiday Monday, June 7, and would prove to be the Fab Four's last session to be recorded exclusively for BBC radio, despite promises to the contrary.

Beatles honored by The Queen

Opposite and left: As the Beatles arrived at Twickenham Film Studios on the morning of June 12 for an early viewing of *Help!*, they were to discover, much to their surprise, that they had each been awarded Membership of the Most Excellent Order of the British Empire, or the MBE. It was the first time that the press had been allowed to publish details of the Queen's Birthday Honors list in advance, and the boys soon found themselves facing a barrage of questions from journalists from around the globe.

Initially, they were somewhat embarrassed, and decided not to accept the award, although Brian Epstein would convince them to change their minds. While public reaction to the announcement was divided, the press response was largely negative, if not downright contemptuous at times. Perhaps the most surprising reaction, however, came from a number of war veterans, who returned their own MBEs in disgust.

North American tour

Above: In mid-June Paul recorded "Yesterday," which was essentially a solo composition, although Brian Epstein would not allow it be billed as such. A string quartet was drafted in for the recording session—the first time strings would feature on a Beatles record. "Yesterday" would not be released as a single in the UK until after the demise of the Beatles—nevertheless it won an Ivor Novello Award for Outstanding Song of the Year. The ceremony was held at the Savoy Hotel. London, on July 13; Paul was the only Beatle to attend. The band was honored with a total of five awards.

Opposite: Exactly a month later, on the same day that the *Help!* LP was released in the States, the boys flew to the US to begin another tour. On the day after their arrival they recorded an appearance for *The Ed Sullivan Show*, before launching their tour the following day with a performance in front of a record 55,000 people at Shea Stadium, New York.

Ten cities in two weeks

Opposite and above: The Beatles' 1965 North American tour was short in comparison to that of the previous year, taking in just ten cities in around two weeks, rather than the grueling 24 cities in a month that they had undertaken in 1964. But this time the venues would be vast, which in itself was a draining experience, for the boys had long tired of having their music drowned out by the screams of their fans. However, the record share of the box-office takings that they would receive was no doubt something of a sweetener. For example, the band could expect to share over $150,000 just for the two shows that they gave at White Sox Park, Chicago, on August 20, which were attended by a total of over 60,000 fans. By now the Beatles were undeniably the biggest recording artists on the planet, bigger even than their hero Elvis, whom they would finally meet ahead of their shows at the Hollywood Bowl.

Meeting The King

Above and opposite: During the North American tour, the Beatles had spent time between shows relaxing with Bob Dylan, The Ronettes, The Supremes, The Byrds, and Carl Wilson and Mike Love of The Beach Boys. However, they had longed to meet Elvis since their first visit to the US back in February 1964, and on August 27, 1965, with the tour beginning to draw to a close, that dream would become a reality, when the Beatles were invited to Elvis's Hollywood home.

Unfortunately, the meeting did not prove to be as convivial as had perhaps been expected, with a combination of nerves and arrogance, particularly on the part of John Lennon, making for a rather uncomfortable evening. Eventually all parties relaxed enough to enjoy an impromptu jam session, which included a few Elvis numbers, before concluding with a rendition of the Beatles' "I Feel Fine."

Receiving their MBEs

Opposite: When the Beatles arrived back on British soil from their American tour, touching down at London Airport on September 2, it was clear that they were relieved to be home. Once again the tour had spawned some chaotic scenes, such as the boys being ferried into Shea Stadium in an armored car, and John having the cap stolen from his head during the final performance at Cow Palace, San Francisco. But the Beatles could now enjoy a six-week break before returning to the studio, when they would begin work on the *Rubber Soul* album.

Right: On October 26, the Beatles, and their guest Brian Epstein, attended Buckingham Palace in order to collect their MBEs.

The Music of Lennon and McCartney

Above and opposite: At the beginning of November the Beatles spent two days at Granada Television Studios in Manchester, recording a special program, *The Music of Lennon and McCartney*, which would celebrate the achievements of Britain's foremost young song-writing talents. The hour-long show included the Beatles miming to both sides of their latest single, their first double A-side, "Day Tripper" and "We Can Work It Out." It also featured appearances from numerous other artists, who performed renditions of Lennon-McCartney compositions, including Lulu singing "From Me To You," Peter and Gordon with "A World Without Love," Cilla Black with "It's For You," and Peter Sellers, who would supply a comedy version of "A Hard Day's Night," delivered in the style of Sir Laurence Olivier performing Shakespeare. Back in London at EMI Studios a few days later, the Beatles recorded "What Goes On," which featured Ringo on lead vocals, and would give him his first writing credit.

Rubber Soul

Above and opposite: Recording sessions for the *Rubber Soul* LP continued in earnest throughout the first half of November, so that the finished album might be available in the record shops in time for Christmas. Despite the rush to complete the LP some individual songs had more time lavished on their recording and production than had been spent on the Beatles' entire first album, and *Rubber Soul* would come to be regarded as a landmark for the band.

1965 was the last year in which the Beatles would manage to release more than one new studio album—as the Fab Four increasingly began to dedicate themselves to studio-craft. Work on the album completed, the Beatles took part in promotional duties, including this photo-shoot in Hampstead, London, where they enjoyed dismantling the polystyrene set at the end of the session.

The final British tour

Opposite: On December 3, the same day that both *Rubber Soul* and the new single, "Day Tripper"/"We Can Work It Out" were released, the Beatles embarked on a short tour of British cinemas, which would begin in Glasgow, and end just over a week later in Cardiff, having taken in a mere nine venues. Although the boys would embark on a world tour the following year, this brief jaunt around the UK would prove to be the Beatles' final British tour, after a series of planned dates was canceled in the spring of 1966.

Above: Prior to this, the "Fab Four" were reunited with American soul singer Mary Wells, who had found fame with the song "My Guy" in the summer of 1964, and had supported the Beatles on their fall tour of the UK that year. The Beatles had long admired American soul, and were influential in bringing singers such as Wells, and vocal groups such as The Ronettes, Marvelettes, and Chiffons, to the attention of the British public.

Crafted music

Opposite and above: As 1965 drew to a close, *Rubber Soul* had climbed to the top of the UK charts, where it would remain for some nine weeks, and it was also poised to top the *Billboard* album chart in the US, where it had already been certified as a million-seller. It was perhaps telling however, that the Beatles were to perform just two songs from the new album during their December dates in Britain; "If I needed Someone" and "Nowhere Man." As the band became more musically ambitious, it would become increasingly difficult for them to replicate on stage the complex, multi-layered compositions that they were producing in the studio environment. However, there was also a question of desire, for the boys were essentially longing for a respite from punishing tours where their carefully crafted music was inaudible above the din of the audience and they had to run the gauntlet of hysterical fans at every performance.

George and Pattie marry

Opposite: At the start of the year "We Can Work It Out" was riding high at the top of the US charts while the B-side "Daytripper" was also listed separately in fifth position. Once the *Christmas Show* had finished, the Beatles had some unaccustomed free time. The grueling "one-night stand" nature of the tours that had been undertaken the previous year were beginning to tell on the band with George particularly feeling the effects. However, his spirits were lifted when he married Pattie Boyd (above) on January 21 in a small wedding ceremony at the Epsom Register Office. The occasion was actually kept so quiet that John and Cynthia were on vacation in Trinidad with Ringo and Maureen at the time but Paul and Brian Epstein were present to share the duty of Best Man. Two weeks later the newly-weds set off to honeymoon in Barbados leaving many female fans dismayed to find that a third member of their beloved band had tied the knot.

Abracadabra: it's Revolver

Opposite and above: The band were soon back in the studio recording "Paperback Writer" and "Rain" for their forthcoming single. Their original intention had been to spend the spring working on another film but unable to find a suitable script they chose to record the next album. The result was *Revolver* which they had originally planned to call *Abracadabra* until it was realized that the name had already been used. It is regarded as an album on which all four members produced their best pieces but sadly it was also the last that they worked on co-operatively and in unison. John's contributions were "And Your Bird Can Sing," "I'm Only Sleeping," and the finale "Tomorrow Never Knows." Paul wrote "For No One," "Here, There, and 'Everywhere" and the much acclaimed "Eleanor Rigby" and George also composed three tracks: "Taxman," "Love You Too," and "I Want To Tell You." Ringo provided the vocals for the next single "Yellow Submarine" and produced the finest drumming performance of his Beatles' career.

Innovation in the studio

Right: John and George in playful mood during a studio session. *Revolver* was an innovative collection of songs which were recorded using new production techniques that distorted normal musical sounds. It was also said to be littered with subtle references to drugs, largely influenced by the group's exposure to LSD. Paul had been the last band member to try the psychedelic drug and the line "I was alone, I took a ride," in "Got To Get You Into My Life" is thought to refer directly to an LSD trip.

Opposite: John had originally penned "Tomorrow Never Comes" without a title but once again a Ringo malapropism provided an appropriate name. It was the first track they recorded for the album and John wanted to sound like the Dalai Lama singing in the mountains. To achieve this his vocals were wired through a Leslie speaker and then re-recorded as they came out of the revolving cabinet to create a vibrato effect.

Last UK live performance

Left and opposite: Shades for Paul McCartney as he and the band made an outside recording in May 1966.

The group had not played live in Britain since December the previous year and what turned out to be the last Beatles British live performance took place on May 1, 1966 at the Empire Pool, Wembley. They were making their fourth appearance in the *New Musical Express* Annual Poll-Winners' All-Star Concert and completed a set lasting fifteen minutes including "Daytripper" and "I Feel Fine." Along with the Rolling Stones they topped the bill that night with the media inventing stories of rivalry between the two bands—a complete fallacy as the two groups often helped out with each other's music. Only three weeks after the concert the Lennons were out on the town with Mick Jagger and Chrissie Shrimpton.

For the Beatles this performance marked the end of the road, and considering this was to be their last public farewell in the UK it was to a very small audience.

Promoting new records

Above and opposite: The Beatles in the grounds of Chiswick House in West London as they made a promotional film, directed by Michael Lindsay-Hogg, for their forthcoming single "Paperback Writer" and "Rain." The previous year the band had decided to produce its own promotional material rather than use television appearances to advertise their new releases. The final scenes of the film were recorded indoors.

Paul had written the A-side and used his new Rickenbacker bass during the recording sessions. The band then experimented by using the bass speaker as a microphone to boost the bass sound; a move that was not popular with the EMI management, as they believed excess bass would cause the stylus to jump on a record. John's "Rain" on the B-side used some of the earlier lyrics played backwards while the rhythm track was slowed to create its pounding sound.

Musical development

Opposite: As the Beatles continued to develop their musical style they also began to use more classical instruments in their compositions. Earlier works such as "Yesterday" had used stringed instruments but on the recording of "For No One" Paul asked Alan Civil to play the French horn solo. Ever diverse in their thinking, the boys also continued to play around with special effects to create the sound they envisaged. A raucous afternoon was spent recording "Yellow Submarine" when a host of extras including Pattie Boyd and Marianne Faithfull rattled chains, clinked glasses and any other props they could lay their hands on to create the record's unique cacophony of noise. Determined to prove their versatility the group paired this song with the haunting "Eleanor Rigby" on the next single, due for release in August.

Above: A photographic session during which the band posed amid rolls of colored wallpaper.

Perfecting compositions

Opposite: Final touches are made to "Paperback Writer"/"Rain" back at the Abbey Road studios. The single was released in the UK on June 10 but proved to be the first Beatles' record since "She Loves You" to reach only No.2 in the British charts a week after its release, losing out to Frank Sinatra's "Strangers in the Night." By 1966 the Beatles were no longer trying to make so many records and were spending more time away from Abbey Road. Their music had increased in sophistication and complexity and they also had the freedom to spend time perfecting their compositions until they were totally happy with the final result. It eventually took ten weeks to record *Revolver* and consequently the final album was packed with sixteen high-quality songs.

Above: In mid-June the band began work on Paul's composition "Here, There And Everywhere." Around this time it was revealed in *The Times* that Paul had just bought a farm on the Mull of Kintyre in Scotland.

Top of the Pops

Opposite and above: Circular lights provided the backdrop for the band during their appearance on *Top of the Pops*. When Epstein realized that "Paperback Writer" had not made the top slot immediately he sprung into action rejecting his original intention to focus on promotional films and organized the band's appearance on *Top of the Pops*. They appeared live in the final slot and as a result reached the top of the charts a week later, remaining there for two weeks. After their television appearance the boys returned to Abbey Road that evening and worked on album tracks until the early hours of the morning.

Back on the world stage

Above and opposite: On June 22, 1966 the Beatles finished their last recording session for the album and the following day flew into Munich for the first leg of a tour that would cover West Germany, Japan, and the Philippines. However, they had had little time to rehearse and during their first house at the Circus Krone in Munich (above) actually stopped playing in the middle of "I'm Down" to agree on the lyrics. The next concert was filmed by German television for a program due for broadcast the following month called

Die Beatles. They then traveled onto Essen for a couple of houses and afterwards returned to Hamburg for the first time since 1962, traveling on a train used by Queen Elizabeth II the previous year (opposite). Arriving at the station at 6 am it took a motorcade of twelve policemen on motorbikes and eight cars to escort them to the Ernst Merck Halle where they played two houses to a total of 11,000 devoted fans. Afterwards they visited their old stamping grounds in the Reeperbahn, the center of Hamburg's nightlife.

Heading for Japan

Above: Ringo and John on board the flight to Tokyo wearing their Happi coats, courtesy of the airline. From Germany the band flew to Japan via London although had to stop in Alaska unexpectedly for 24 hours due to typhoon warnings.

Opposite: John Lennon gazes out of the band's Tokyo hotel room. At Haneda Airport in Tokyo 1500 fans were waiting to greet them and despite attempts to keep their hotel location a secret, the local radio station found them and tracked their every move making them virtual prisoners in their hotel. The band were booked to play five shows at the Nippon Budokan Hall. The hall was a sacred building for sumo wrestlers, although the Beatles had been totally unaware of the building's significance, and the choice of venue shocked and angered many Japanese, resulting in the introduction of additional security measures to protect the band.

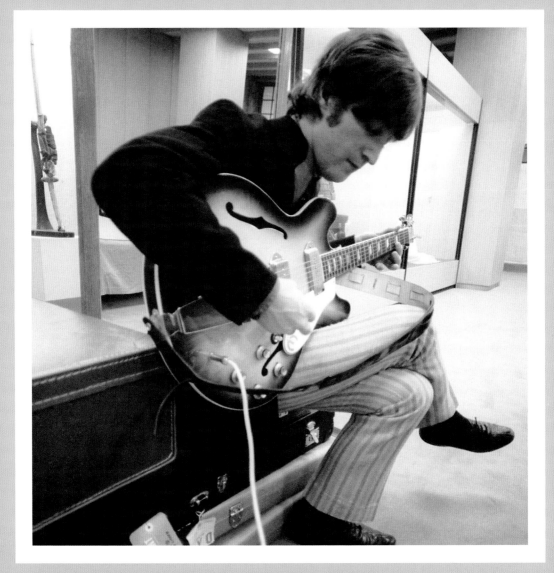

Death threats

Opposite: John strumming his Epiphone Casino backstage. Each Japanese concert attracted an audience of 10,000 but 3,000 policemen were employed to keep order throughout the venues, contributing to the subdued response from the fans that also showed up the band's below par performance. The Beatles had received death threats due to the choice of venue and eventually raced through their numbers to get off the stage safely.

Above: Boredom had well and truly set in at their Japanese hotel room. The last shows at the Budokan were recorded in color and eventually edited together to produce an hour-long special called *The Beatles Recital*, From Nippon Budokan that was screened by NTV Channel 4.

Playing Nippon Budokan

Opposite and above: The Beatles run on stage for their matinee performance at the Nippon Budokan. After the three-day run of shows in Japan the band then flew on to play in the Philippines and they soon realized on landing that there would be no special treatment. They were greeted by aggressive military police and were kept on a boat for several hours, separated from their luggage and management team.

They were booked to play two houses but chaos reigned when they were told they were late for a reception at the presidential palace organized by the first lady, Imelda Marcos. Epstein had refused the invitation knowing that the boys disliked formal parties but television footage had been shown assuring viewers and the waiting crowds that the Beatles would soon appear; but they did not show. Claims that they had snubbed the first family dominated the media the next day and the Beatles had all their protection withdrawn as they faced angry rebukes at Manila Airport. The fact that more than 80,000 people had attended the concerts now seemed irrelevant.

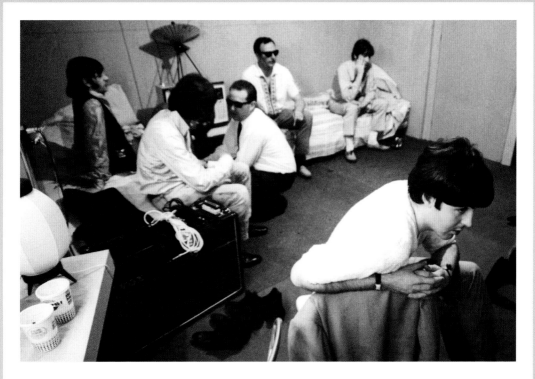

Beatles banned

Opposite: A quick backstage rehearsal for John and George. Further problems were to come when, at the end of July and two weeks before their next American tour, John's interview with Maureen Cleave originally covered by the *Evening Standard* in London was reprinted in the US teenage magazine *Datebook*. The interview had at first seemed fairly innocuous covering John's interest in cars and natural history but then he was quoted as saying "Christianity will go. It will vanish and it will shrink... We're more popular than Jesus now. I don't know which will go first, rock 'n' roll or Christianity." As a direct response many radio stations in the South banned their music and there were public burnings of their records in the streets.

Above: In America many less zealous church leaders tried to calm the situation but John, Epstein, and press officer Tony Barrow quickly hatched a plan to limit the damage that had been caused. The possibility of canceling the tour was unfeasible and instead John held a press conference at Chicago's Astor Towers on August 11. There John made a long, rather complex speech defending his remarks saying "I wasn't saying whatever they are saying I was saying. I was sort of deploring the attitude towards Christianity. I'm sorry, I'm sorry. I'm sorry I said it really. I never meant it as a religious thing." Memories were to prove short and apart from the odd demonstration the fans were as devoted as ever.

Backstage

Above and opposite: The band wait backstage at a concert venue. After the events in Asia, and the negative publicity prior to their arrival in America and the Far East, the Beatles were obviously less than enthusiastic about the coming tour and were very lethargic in their plans for the forthcoming concerts. They made no attempt to play any of the tracks from *Revolver*, instead falling back on original work that needed little rehearsal. Despite this it was highly successful tour but concerts were no longer sold out. The fans were still there and passionately loyal, but starting to decrease in numbers.

An end to touring

Left: John pictured after the press conference at the Astor Towers. Security proved to be a continuous headache during their US tour. In Cleveland 2,500 fans began to swarm toward the stage and with their safety under threat, the boys dropped their instruments and fled. In Cincinnati they were expected to play under a flimsy piece of canvas during a violent rainstorm. Only after Paul was physically sick at the prospect was the performance abandoned until the following day.

Opposite: The Beatles, summer 1966. By the time they reached California for the concert at Candlestick Park on August 29, the boys had decided that nine years of touring, playing in excess of 1,400 live performances was enough and made it their last ever gig. To mark the occasion Tony Barrow, their press officer, made an audiocassette recording while John and Paul took photographs on stage. When all the equipment was finally packed away George was quoted as saying "That's it, I'm not a Beatle anymore." In their heady early days the boys had enjoyed the live performances, often playing to small houses and bantering with the audience. From there they had moved onto fame and fortune touring across the world but it had taken its toll and they were now determined to work purely in the studio where they could focus upon their music.

How I Won The War

Left: In the fall of 1966 the group gained the much-needed space to spread their wings and develop their own personal lives and careers. On his return from America John flew to Hanover in West Germany where he had been contracted to play Private Gripweed, a part created for him, in *How I Won The War*. George could at last follow his growing passion for Indian religion and culture. Of the four he had become disillusioned with the Beatle lifestyle the most quickly. In India he studied the sitar under Ravi Shankar and developed his skills as a composer, determined to introduce the instrument into future Beatles' work. Paul soon embarked on a solo project composing the musical score for the film *The Family Way* and then flew out to Kenya with Jane Asher in November. Ringo took the opportunity to go on vacation to Malaga in Spain with Maureen.

Opposite: At the end of the year John appeared in the *Not Only...But Also* Christmas special with Peter Cook and Dudley Moore, taking a cameo role as the doorman of a "members only" gentlemen's public lavatory. He had just met Yoko Ono for the first time when he attended a private viewing of her art exhibition at the Indica gallery in London. By now his marriage to Cynthia was under a great deal of strain but it was to be a while before he began his relationship with Yoko.

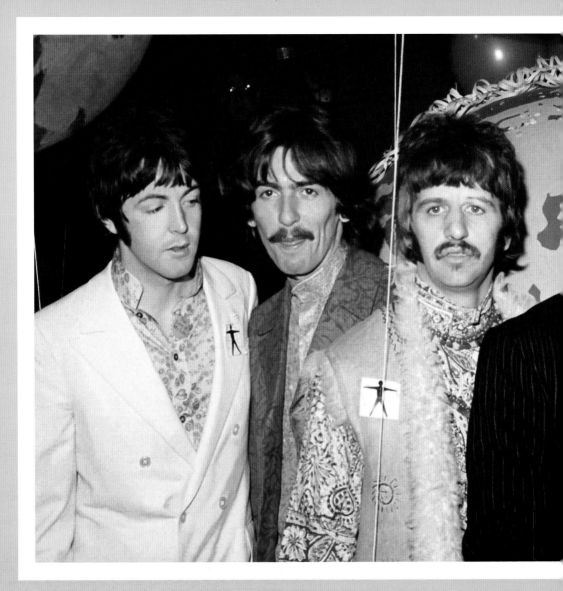

Part Two

A Long and Winding Road

A new contract with EMI

Opposite: John captured during a recording session. In January the Beatles signed a new contract with EMI destined to last until January 1976. They began the studio sessions for the forthcoming album *Sgt. Pepper's Lonely Hearts Club Band* on February 1 starting with the title song "Sgt. Pepper's Lonely Hearts Club Band" followed two days later by "A Day In The Life." This song was written by Lennon and McCartney and proved to be a testimony to their partnership with Paul writing the middle and John completing the beginning and end. Paul was determined to expand the use of classical instruments and wanted a full symphony orchestra to play on the track, employing forty musicians at a cost of £367.

Right: George had recently returned from his six-week vacation in India and, knowing that he had discovered his spiritual home, found it very difficult to return to being a Beatle. Studio recording often meant adding layers onto tracks and he was often redundant, as guitars were not always used. Only one of his compositions "Within You Without You" was included on the album and Harrison was the sole performer. It took the boys 700 hours to record the album, at a cost of £25,000, which was a phenomenal amount of time compared with a normal production schedule in the mid-sixties, especially given that their first LP had been completed in ten hours.

Paul, Jane, and Linda

Left Paul met girlfriend Jane Asher at London Airport after she returned from touring in America. In 1967 Paul had spent an evening at the Bag o' Nails club watching Georgie Fame. There he met Eric Burdon, lead singer with the Animals who was accompanied by Linda Eastman, a photographer who was trying to extend her portfolio of pop stars. Paul and Linda met again four days later (opposite) at the press launch party for *Sgt. Pepper* where the couple were soon observed deep in conversation. Jane Asher was touring in the States with the Old Vic at the time, but the relationship between Paul and Jane was already beginning to founder.

In February the next single "Penny Lane"/ "Strawberry Fields Forever" was released but failed to reach No.1 in the UK, overtaken by a song from Humperbert Engeldinck, as John loved to call him.

Recording Sgt. Pepper

Above: The band in Hyde Park, London. While recording the *Sgt. Pepper* album John and Paul addressed the need for a track for Ringo. After throwing several ideas into the pot a set of lyrics was finally written to a McCartney composition. Originally called "Bad Finger Boogie" the song "With A Little Help From My Friends" finally emerged and became one of the classic tracks from the album. Its popularity still continues today and it has been covered by a number of artists including Joe Cocker in 1968 and Wet Wet Wet in 1988.

Opposite: The band pose for photographers outside Brian Epstein's house in Belgravia.

Peter Blake's iconic album cover

Above and opposite: The band chose the press launch party, held at Brian Epstein's home in Belgravia, to reveal the cover for *Sgt. Pepper's Lonely Hearts Club Band*. Once the recording was well under way the band had turned their attention to the packaging for the LP and had been introduced to artist Peter Blake by the cover's art director Robert Fraser. Paul worked closely with Blake to explain his ideas and the concept of a tableau emerged. Blake used the mannequins from Madame Tussauds and surrounded the Beatles with life-size cut-outs of over seventy famous people chosen by the band as their "heroes," including Bob Dylan, Marilyn Monroe and Oscar Wilde. Two weeks were spent arranging the scene at photographer Michael Cooper's studio in Chelsea. The bill for the cover was £2,800, an huge amount in an era when the budget for an album cover was usually around £100. The band also broke with tradition and decided they wanted a gatefold sleeve and the song lyrics printed on the cover. Despite the misgivings of EMI and Epstein the cover won a Grammy and proved to be the perfect accompaniment to the innovative music on the album within.

One million advance orders in the US

Opposite and above: The band celebrates the completion of the album during the launch party. *Sgt. Pepper's Lonely Hearts Club Band* was released in the UK on June 1, 1967, selling a quarter of a million copies in the first week alone. The following day it was released in the States, where it had already clocked up over one million advance orders. Nine days after its British release it reached No.1 in the album charts and remained there for a solid twenty-three weeks.

Using the De Lane Lea Studios, the band had already started recording the next album, *Magical Mystery Tour*. Again an orchestra was used to record "All You Need Is Love," destined to be the final track and on June 25 the band sang this Lennon and McCartney composition on a BBC program called *Our World*.

All You Need Is Love

Opposite and right: The band preparing for the live satellite transmission of *Our World*. At the final rehearsal it was agreed they needed an audience to create a party atmosphere so the band rounded up several celebrity friends including Eric Clapton, Keith Moon, Mick Jagger, and Marianne Faithfull to make a "singalong" backing chorus. During the final performance the orchestra wore full evening dress, the Beatles were seated on stools and their celebrity "audience" sat on the floor around them.

This performance proved to be the band's last live recording. "All You Need Is Love" along with the flip-side "Baby You're A Rich Man" was released as a single the following month, once again fast-tracking its way to the top of the charts on both sides of the Atlantic. To this day "All You Need Is Love" and *Sgt. Pepper's Lonely Hearts Club Band* remain synonymous with the flower-power image of the summer of 1967.

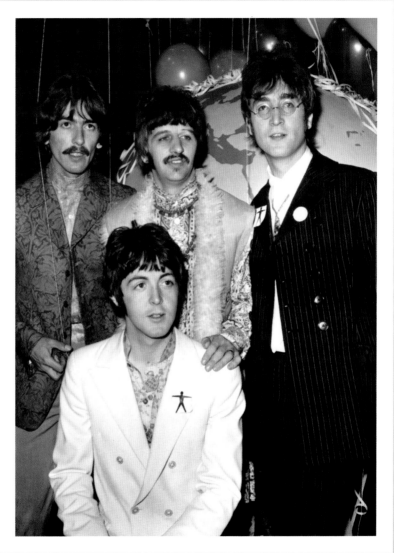

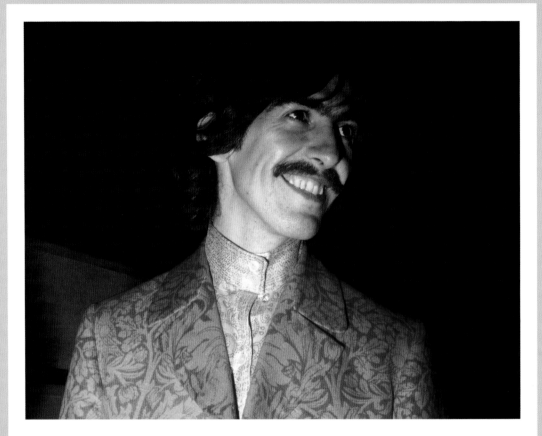

Our World

Above: George Harrison captured during rehearsals for the BBC's *Our World*. The live program was destined to be transmitted via satellite to twenty-four countries in five continents, reaching an estimated audience of 300 million. The concept behind the program was for each country to have a five-minute window "bringing man face to face with mankind" so the band were tasked with writing a song with simple lyrics and a melody that would appeal worldwide. It was John who came up with the catchy song — "All You Need Is love."

Opposite: The band rehearsing with the multi-lingual sandwich boards used for the live performance. The song had taken ten days to record for the album but the boys then had the huge task of recreating the sound in a live recording and so George Martin wisely insisted they use a backing track.

Another ban

Left: Paul holds John's son Julian during a vacation in Greece. John was keen to purchase an island retreat and the group came very close to purchasing the island of Leslo for £90,000 but pulled out in the last stages of negotiation.

Opposite: Paul holds up a newspaper with the headline news about Keith Richard's and Mick Jagger's recent drugs case. That summer the group became more open about their drug-taking. During an interview Paul was confronted about his usage and he decided to openly admit that he had taken LSD, trying to justify his actions with what he perceived to be a rational argument. In July the group signed a petition in *The Times* which called for the legalisation of marijuana. Their names were printed alongside those of many other celebrities in a full-page article and it was this attention in the press that led the authorities to look for any references to drugs in the lyrics in the *Sgt. Pepper* album. The BBC banned "Lucy In The Sky With Diamonds" based on the song's initials alone although the inspiration for the title had come from a picture drawn by John's son, Julian.

Meeting the Maharishi

Above and opposite: The Beatles and friends pictured with the Maharishi in August 1967.

Pattie had recently attended a lecture at Caxton Hall on Spiritual Regeneration, led by a disciple of Maharishi Mahesh Yogi and introduced the idea to her husband and the other Beatles. George, who was still seeking enlightenment and becoming disenchanted with drugs, John, and Paul all decided to attend a lecture at the London Hilton given by the Maharishi at the end of the month. The Maharishi had formed the International Meditation Society in 1959 and his organization provided a chance for westerners to follow his spiritual pathway for the price of a large membership fee. His timing was perfect and he successfully enticed many followers with messages of peace and love. Ringo, who had been unable to attend the lecture as Maureen had just given birth, then joined the other band members for a seminar held in Bangor, where they learned the principles of Transcendental Meditation.

Brian Epstein dies

Above: The Beatles aboard the *Magical Mystery Tour* bus. Earlier in the year Brian Epstein had a premonition that he was going to die and on August 27 was found dead at his home in Belgravia at the age of thirty-two. He had been suffering from depression and the cause of death was found to be an accidental drugs overdose. His funeral was held two days later in Liverpool but was only for close family, with none of the band attending. The band met together to plan their future and decided that they needed some "normality" after

Brian's sudden death. It was agreed that the filming of the proposed *Magical Mystery Tour* should go ahead post-haste. After finding a soundman and three cameramen they searched the actors' directory *Spotlight* and chose thirty-three people to make up the rest of the cast. The tour bus set off from Baker Street in London and collected the band members, including Paul (opposite), along the way, traveling via Virginia Water in Surrey, then on to Basingstoke for lunch before arriving at the Royal Hotel in Teignmouth, where they stayed the night.

Filming in the West Country

Left: George Harrison talking to delighted fans when the tour reached Torquay in Devon. After traveling for a total of five days they discovered they were short of usable material and would need to supplement the footage. Unable to find a vacant studio at such short notice they made use of an old US base at West Malling, near Maidstone, that was suitable.

Opposite: John and George "on set" in Newquay. The work was edited using ten hours of filming to create just fifty-two minutes for the final version. When it was screened on television at the end of December the film was heavily criticized, although over the years this view has changed, with many now expressing admiration for the Beatles' first project without Epstein's guidance.

Magical Mystery Tour

Above: From 1966 onwards Paul McCartney was the main force behind the singles released by the band. He was also the chief inspiration behind *Sgt. Pepper* and *Magical Mystery Tour* and generally decided the direction in which the band should travel. John seemed to have relinquished his position as the father of the band, although he still produced the occasional timeless classic such as "I Am The Walrus." John later claimed it was his own personal favorite and enjoyed the way his lyrics had confused many academics.

Opposite: John advises some of the extras in Newquay. On each side of the Atlantic the record companies debated how to sell the *Magical Mystery Tour* songs. There were six tracks from the film so in the States Capitol decided to add some of that year's single releases to make album while in Britain EMI opted for an extended EP, although the album was eventually released in Britain in 1976.

The Beatles form Apple

Left: George and "Magic" Alex on board the tour bus. In the spring of 1967, the Beatles were advised by their accountants to form a new company that would give them some protection from their hefty tax liabilities. The name Apple was chosen and after bouncing around many different ideas , the Apple boutique opened on December 7, 1967. However, the venture was to prove disastrous, lasting only eight months. The one success from their new company was Apple Music; all the other projects they initiated merely drained the bank balance.

Opposite: The band photographed in their hotel room while on location. The single "Hello Goodbye"/"I am The Walrus," recorded for the *Magical Mystery Tour* album, was always destined to be the next hit. It rapidly shot to the top of the UK charts, remaining there for seven weeks, also becoming the band's fourth Christmas No. 1 in five years. *The Magical Mystery Tour* EP held the second chart position and with "I Am The Walrus" also on the EP it rather uniquely held first and second place.

Acting naturally

Opposite: The band relaxing at Plymouth Hoe during a press call. By the end of the year all four members of the band had actively pursued their own interests. Following in Paul's (pictured above with his father Jim) footsteps George had been asked to write the soundtrack for the film *Wonderwall* while Ringo decided that he would join John in the world of acting. Playing the part of Emmanuel, a Mexican gardener, he appeared in the film *Candy* alongside Richard Burton, Walter Matthau, and Marlon Brando. Starr had always been a natural actor in the Beatles' films and was only too willing to join such a prestigious cast.

Meditating in India

Above: The Beatles had planned to travel to India in 1967 but postponed the visit after Brian's sudden death. In February 1968, freed up from recording commitments, they decided to spend three months at the Maharishi's International Academy of Transcendental Meditation in Rishikesh. John and George, the two members of the band who were most committed to the concept, set off first with their wives. Ringo and Paul with their partners followed but Ringo and Maureen, disliking the food and climate, quickly returned to England. Paul stayed for five weeks but mainly because it gave him the space to compose his music. John and George stayed on, attending the daily lectures and relishing the simple lifestyle. Eight weeks into the Transcendental Meditation course rumors were circulating about the Maharishi's relationships with some of the women students. John and several others challenged him and then left the academy swiftly without completing the course. On his return John penned a song criticizing their latest guru but changed the title from "Maharishi" to "Sexy Sadie" to avoid litigation.

Opposite: John and Ringo pay a visit backstage at the Adelphi Theatre to see fellow Liverpudlian Gerry Marsden.

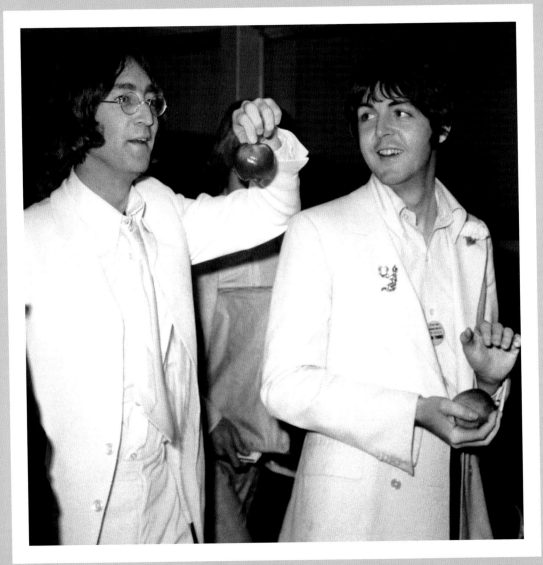

A new direction

Opposite: In May 1968 John and Paul, carrying apples, flew to the States for five days. The purpose of their visit was to promote the band's new business venture, Apple Corps, but Paul also took the opportunity to meet up once again with Linda Eastman. In the summer Apple Records was also created and the company signed its first new "talent," James Taylor.

Right: In the same month George and Pattie set off for Nice to attend the Cannes Film Festival where Ringo and Maureen joined them to watch the première of George's film *Wonderwall*. At Kenwood John and Yoko, who were now spending much more time in each other's company, took advantage of Cynthia's trip to Greece and made several recordings at his home. These were later released on the album *Unfinished Music No.1: Two Virgins*, which featured the naked couple on the cover. When Cynthia returned from her vacation a week later, she found that Yoko had moved in.

The White Album

Opposite: John and George at the opening of Apple Tailoring in Chelsea. By May 1968 the band were beginning work on recordings for the forthcoming *White Album* but discord was starting to set in. John invited Yoko to the sessions despite the rest of the band's unhappiness at this arrangement and on June 9 John and Paul actually worked in separate studios for the first time: John was developing "Revolution 9" while Paul worked on "Blackbird". The band had plenty of material for the album but during the twenty weeks it took to record the final product there was constant tension and resentment. Rather than all members of the group having an input into each song the most common practice evolving was for each member to

own a song and use the others to add their pieces. George later commented that this was the time when "the rot began to set in." Despite the stress in the studio *The White Album* was still an unprecedented success with the final 32 tracks covering an incredible array of musical styles. Its stark white cover designed by Richard Hamilton also provided a sharp contrast to the psychedelic *Sgt. Pepper*.

Above: John, George and Paul recording their voices for *Yellow Submarine*, a full-length animated film. The group spent minimal time composing and recording the soundtrack but the final film was an inspiration and has remained a classic.

Changing relationships

Left: In June 1968 George flew to the States to take part in *Raga*, a documentary about the life of Ravi Shankar.

Opposite: John and Yoko were by now inseparable—he even had a bed brought into the studio and gave her a microphone so she could watch and make comments. After a particularly strained recording session in August Ringo declared his intention to leave the band and promptly went on vacation, spending two weeks on Peter Sellers' yacht. Throughout the time the album was recorded, members of the band frequently disappeared to pursue their own interests, leaving the others to carry on without them. Ringo came back to the studio in early September but this reunion was merely papering over the cracks.

John and Yoko in the dock

Above: In the fall of 1968 John and Yoko were charged with possession of cannabis. After the hearing at Marylebone Crown Court they were remanded on bail and the following month John was convicted and fined £150. Yoko had recently announced she was pregnant but in November lost the baby after a miscarriage.

Opposite: John, Yoko, and Brian Jones with John's son Julian at the press conference for the Rolling Stones' *Rock & Roll Circus* television special in which John made a guest appearance.

During the sessions for the forthcoming album,"Hey Jude," a song written by Paul and dedicated to John's son Julian who was caught up in his parents divorce proceedings, was recorded. This timeless piece lasting in excess of seven minutes was first played at Mick Jagger's twenty-fifth-birthday party at the Vesuvio Club. Hitting the top of the charts in eleven countries, it had sold five million copies by the end of the year. *The White Album* was released at the end of November and in the States sold 1.1 million copies in the first five days.

Getting back

Opposite: At the beginning of 1969 the band started recording the *Get Back* documentary. Still tied into a contract set up by Epstein, they agreed to be filmed while they recorded their next album. The main feature would be a 42-minute impromptu performance held on top of the Apple building on January 30. The Beatles played live—for the first time in two-and-a-half years—until police stopped them because they had brought the local traffic to a complete halt. It was to be their very last live performance.

Right: George and Pattie. During the *Get Back* sessions George had become the second member of the band to walk out, this time after an argument with John and Paul. He returned later that evening but the chasm was slowly but surely widening. None of the band was interested in developing the album that accompanied the *Get Back* movie and it was left to Glyn Johns to drive the production. He completed his work by May but the Beatles decided to put the project on hold and move on to *Abbey Road*. It wasn't until Phil Spector worked on the tapes the following year that it metamorphosed in to *Let It Be*, released in May 1970.

Paul weds Linda

Opposite and above: Paul married Linda at Marylebone Register Office in March 1969 with none of the band present. They had decided to marry only a week earlier and it was a very quiet affair with Paul's brother Mike as Best Man. Paul had wanted to employ Linda's father, Lee Eastman, to sort out the band's ailing finances. Eastman sent in his son John, who made many recommendations including the buy-out of NEMS to take control of their back catalog. Although this made financial sense John refused to agree as he thought Paul might gain an unfair advantage in the transaction. He instead opted to employ Allen Klein, renowned for renegotiating contracts, and persuaded Ringo and George to follow suit. Klein improved the deal with EMI but had less success with NEMS, failing to gain control of the back catalog when it was sold to Sir Lew Grade. In July the band agreed to record the album *Abbey Road*, which was an unqualified success despite the ongoing tensions. This was largely due to the quality of the material and the band avoiding each other when necessary. The LP carried two stunning Harrison tracks, "Here Comes The Sun" and "Something," the only Beatles' record released as a single after the album went on sale.

All things must pass

Left and opposite: John and Yoko married in Gibraltar eight days after Paul and Linda. Shortly after the newly-weds installed themselves in Room 902 at the Amsterdam Hilton where they held their seven-day "bed-in" for world peace, amid maximum publicity.

In 1970 the band's two last albums were released. *Let It Be* had been recorded after the *Get Back* documentary but Phil Spector remixed the final product, eliminating the raw sound the album was intended to feature, much to Paul's dismay. "Hey Jude" was also released and included the band's last No.1 single, "The Ballad of John and Yoko."

During the year all four members of the band pursued solo projects. John was immersed in his work with Yoko, Ringo had already begun to record his solo album *Sentimental Journey*, Paul was working on his album *McCartney* and George had toured with Eric Clapton before starting work on his solo album *All Things Must Pass*. The end finally came when Paul announced in the media that he was planning to leave the band. In August, Paul confirmed that the Beatles would never work together again and on New Year's Eve 1970 he filed a petition to dissolve the partnership in the London High Court. The band had finally reached the end of a long and winding road.

Acknowledgements
Thanks to Hayley Newman, Rick Mayston, Patricia Froux-Leaker, Stacey
Smithson, Martina Oliver, Hilary Marsden, Richard Betts, Cliff Salter,
Mel Cox and John Dunne.